The Gigantic Coloring Book of God's World

TYNDALE

Tyndale House Publishers, Inc.
Carol Stream, Illinois

Visit Tyndale's website for kids at www.tyndale.com/kids.

TYNDALE, Tyndale's quill logo, and *Happy Day* are registered trademarks of Tyndale House Publishers, Inc.

The Gigantic Coloring Book of God's World

Copyright © 2010 by Tyndale House Publishers, Inc., Carol Stream, Illinois 60188. All rights reserved.

Originally published by Standard Publishing, Cincinnati, Ohio. First printing by Tyndale House Publishers, Inc., in 2019.

Edited by Ruth Frederick

Illustrations by Janet Skiles, Nan Pollard, Norma Garris, Robin Boyer, David Schimmell, Terry Julien, Lloyd Birmingham, Liz McCleod, Mary Bausman, Nancy Carter, Judy Blankenship, Roberta K. Loman, and Jill Dubin

Scripture taken from the International Children's Bible.® Copyright © 1986, 1988, 1999 by Thomas Nelson, Inc. Used by permission. All rights reserved.

For manufacturing information regarding this product, please call 1-800-323-9400.

For information about special discounts for bulk purchases, please contact Tyndale House Publishers at csresponse@tyndale.com, or call 1-800-323-9400.

ISBN 978-1-4143-9499-2

Printed in the United States of America

25   24   23   22   21   20   19
7   6   5   4   3   2   1

TYNDALE

God's Wonderful World

God made a wonderful world.

God made the land.

He made the sun, the moon, and the stars.

God made all the animals.

Thank you, God, for animals.

God made sheep.

God takes cares of the animals wherever they live.

God made beautiful butterflies.

God made trees and flowers.

God made pumpkins.

"God is truly good."

Psalm 73:1

God made wonderful things to taste.

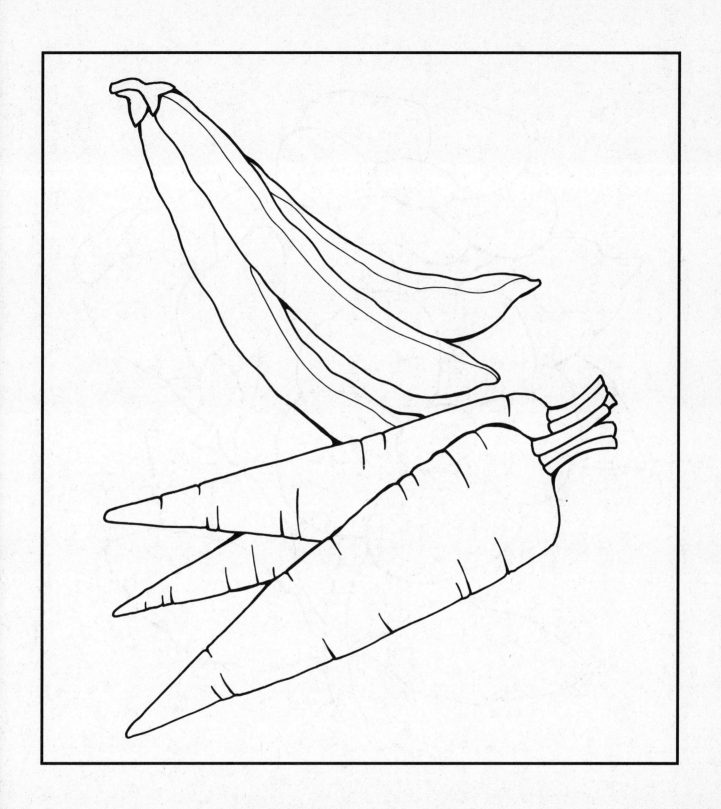

Thank you, God, for good food.

God's world has wonderful things to smell.

Thank you, God, for things to smell.

God made wonderful things to hear.

I can hear music.

Thank you, God, for things to hear.

God made wonderful things to feel.

Thank you, God, for things to feel.

God made people for his wonderful world.

"He made us."

Psalm 100:3

God made mothers.

God made fathers.

God made grandparents.

"Love each other."

John 15:17

God made friends.
Thank you, God, for my friends.

Thank you, God, for people.

"God . . . made the whole world."

Acts 17:24

God Made the Animals

"Let the earth be filled with animals."

God made the turtle.

God made the squirrel.

God made the rabbit.

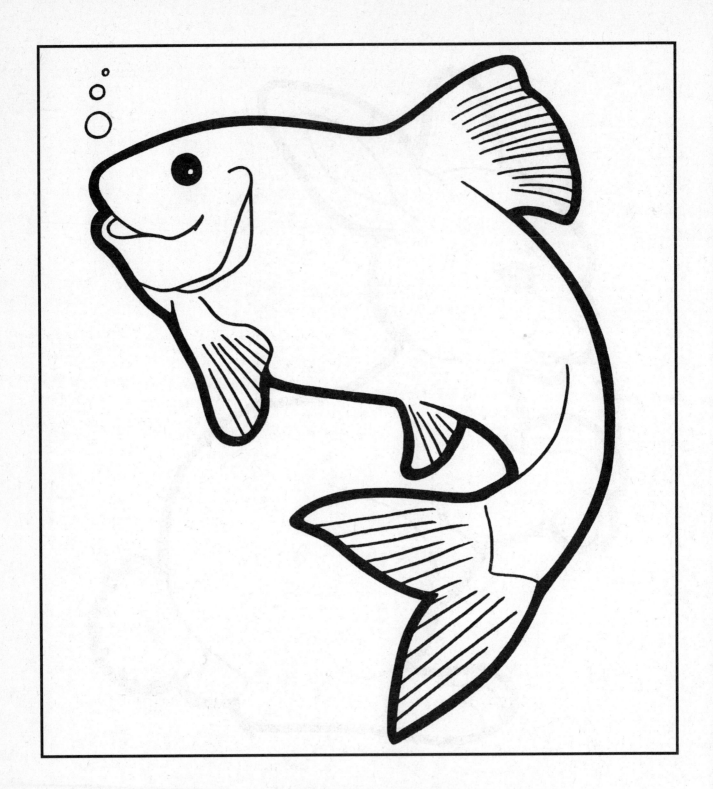

"God . . . created every living thing that moves in the sea."

God made the kitten.

God made the dog.

God made the donkey.

God made the chicken.

God made the cow.

God made the pig.

God made the goat.

God made the horse.

God made the lamb.

"God . . . made every bird that flies."

Genesis 1:21

Noah's Ark Animals

duckling

God sent a big flood.

tortoises

giraffe

God kept the animals safe on Noah's ark.

wolf cubs

"The Lord does great things."

Psalm 111:2

raccoon

There was food for everyone.

bunnies

deer

God took good care of the animals.

elephant

"Depend on the Lord and his strength."

Psalm 105:4

"Every living thing . . . is mine."

Psalm 50:11

lion cub

mice

God is good.

puppy

"The Lord has done great things for us."

Psalm 126:3

lamb

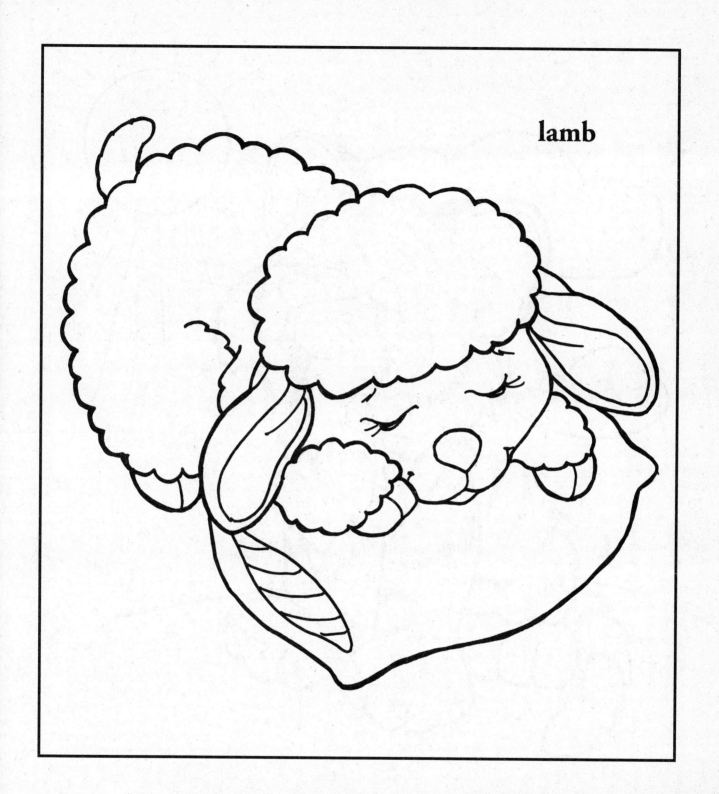

"I go to bed and sleep in peace."

Psalm 4:8

tiger cub

The sun came out. The flood was over.

piglets

Thank you, God!

Baby Animals

A baby deer is called a fawn.

"He made us, and we belong to him."

Psalm 100:3

This baby chick will grow to be a chicken.

A baby opossum is called a joey.

A baby horse is called a foal.

A baby cat is called a kitten.

A baby dog is a pup.

A baby duck is called a duckling.

A baby rabbit is called a bunny.

A baby bear is called a cub.

"Depend on the Lord and his strength."

Psalm 105:4

A baby mouse is called a pinkie.

A baby skunk is called a kit.

I Love You

Loving is taking a walk with a friend.

Loving is sharing.

"Do everything in love."

1 Corinthians 16:14

Love is a family hug.

Love is thinking of others.

Love is saying thank-you.

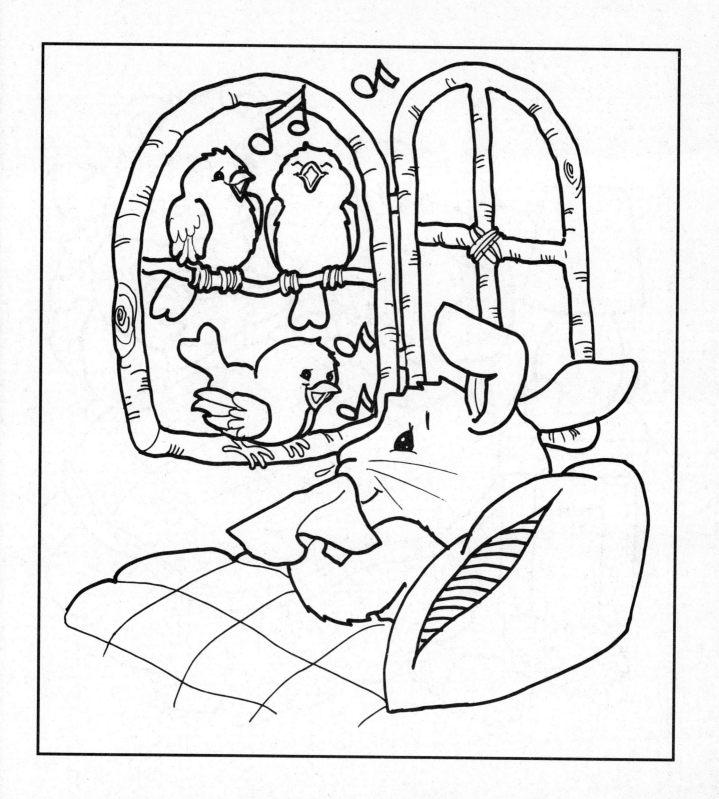

"Love your neighbor."

Matthew 19:19

Love is caring.

Love is listening.

Love is giving a smile.

"Love is patient."

════ *1 Corinthians 13:4* ════

Love is helping.

"Love is . . . kind."

1 Corinthians 13:4

Love is saying "I love you."

"Love never ends."

1 Corinthians 13:8

God's Wild Animals

"God made the wild animals."

Genesis 1:25

God made the elephant.

God made the lion.

God made the tiger.

God made the seal.

God made the alligator.

God made the bear.

God made the penguin.

God made the rhinoceros.

God made the hippopotamus.

God made the walrus.

God made the monkey.

God made the kangaroo.

God made the panda.

"Praise him, you wild animals."

Psalm 148:10

It's Springtime

Spring is here!

Signs of new life are all around.

Spring showers help the flowers grow.

Flowers push up through the ground.

Soon the flowers are smiling at the sun.

"I am putting my rainbow in the clouds."

Genesis 9:13

Springtime is planting time.

Farmers plow and plant their fields.

"There is a time to plant."

Ecclesiastes 3:2

Birds build nests in the springtime.

The mother bird lays her eggs.

She sits on the eggs until they hatch.

"He gives food to every living creature."

Psalm 136:25

At the park, baby ducks go swimming.

**On the farm, baby animals are born.
Thank you, God, for springtime!**

God's Amazing World

The African savannah makes a good home for large plant-eating mammals like zebras.

Underneath the soil of the savannah, colonies of tiny mole rats dig tunnels and eat plant tubers.

**In the hot, dry Sonoran Desert of North
America, a tall saguaro cactus can store
up to a ton of water in its pulp.**

**Moth larvae living inside Mexican jumping beans
make the beans jump in the warm desert sun.**

**Colorful jaguars live in the Amazon
rainforest of South America.**

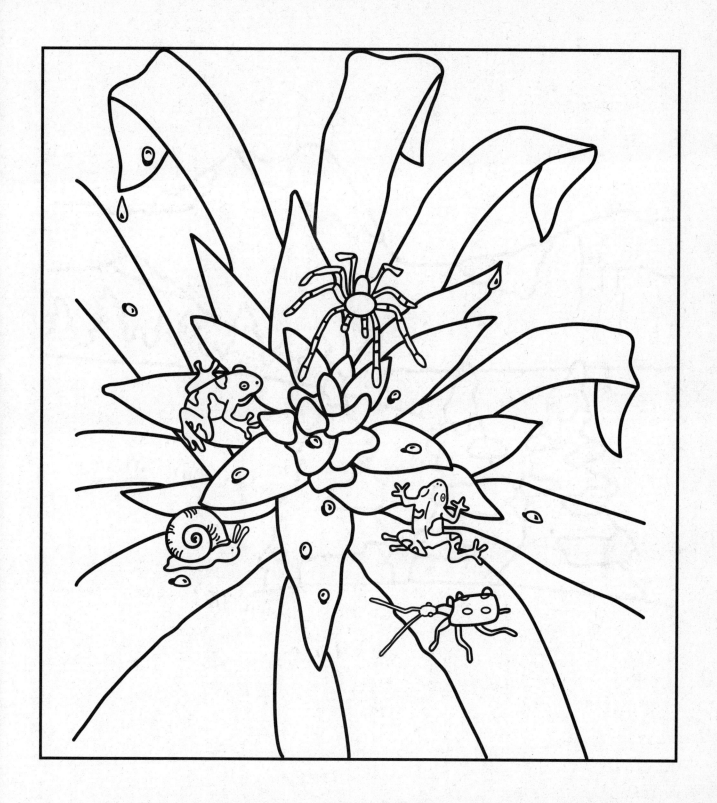

Bromeliad plants catch rainwater and provide a home for beetles, spiders, snails, and frogs.

The arctic tundra has the world's coldest temperatures. The ground freezes except during a short summer season.

Arctic hares, with short ears and very long hind feet, live in the tundra in large groups.

In the deciduous forest, trees turn color in autumn and lose their leaves in winter.

Chipmunks in the forest live in hidden burrows, often inside fallen logs.

"Who sends rain . . . so the grass begins to grow?"

Job 38:27

**Among the prairie grasses grow
many different wildflowers.**

From land, the ocean appears to be nothing but water.

**"God created every living thing . . .
that moves in the sea."**

Genesis 1:21

**God's amazing world is full of surprises,
no matter where you look!**

God's Animals on the Farm

Welcome to the farm!

"A good man takes care of his animals."

Proverbs 12:10

When the sun rises, the rooster crows.
Time to get up!

Many of the breakfast foods we eat come from the farm.
Match each breakfast food to the crop or animal that it comes from.
Thank you, God, for food!

The animals need breakfast too.

The horses love to eat hay and oats.

The farm has a newborn baby!

Oh no! The foal has wandered off, and his mother can't find him. Help the mare find the lost foal.

The pigs like to play in the mud.

"He gives food to cattle."

Psalm 147:9

The rabbit gets a carrot treat.

Taking care of the animals is lots of work!

Who keeps the crows from eating all the corn?
Connect the dots to find out.

Frogs hop and play near the farmer's pond. Ribbit!

**Peacocks show their colors in the yard
of the farmhouse.**

The farm cat gives her kittens a bath
in the sunny barn loft.

**The sheepdog watches the sheep
and keeps them safe.**

The sheep are hiding from the sheepdog.
Can you find the five sheep hidden in this picture?

"Love is patient and kind."

1 Corinthians 13:4

The mama duck takes her ducklings for an afternoon swim. Quack, quack!

When the sun sets, the farm animals go to sleep.

Goodnight, farm!

Thank you, God, for making all the animals on the farm!

Backyard Bugs

Monarch Butterfly

"Lord, you have made many things."

Psalm 104:24

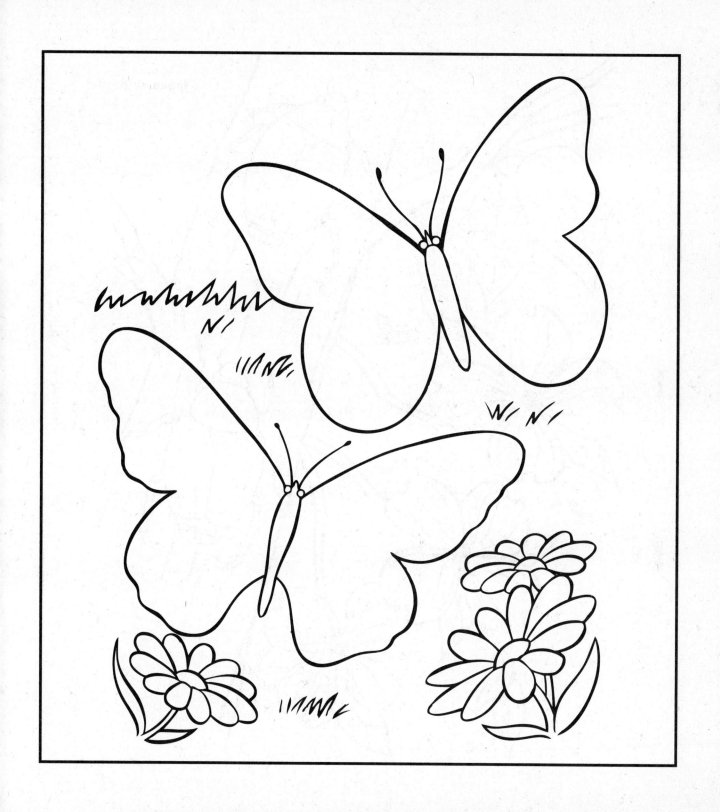

**God made beautiful butterflies. Use your crayon
to decorate these butterfly wings.**

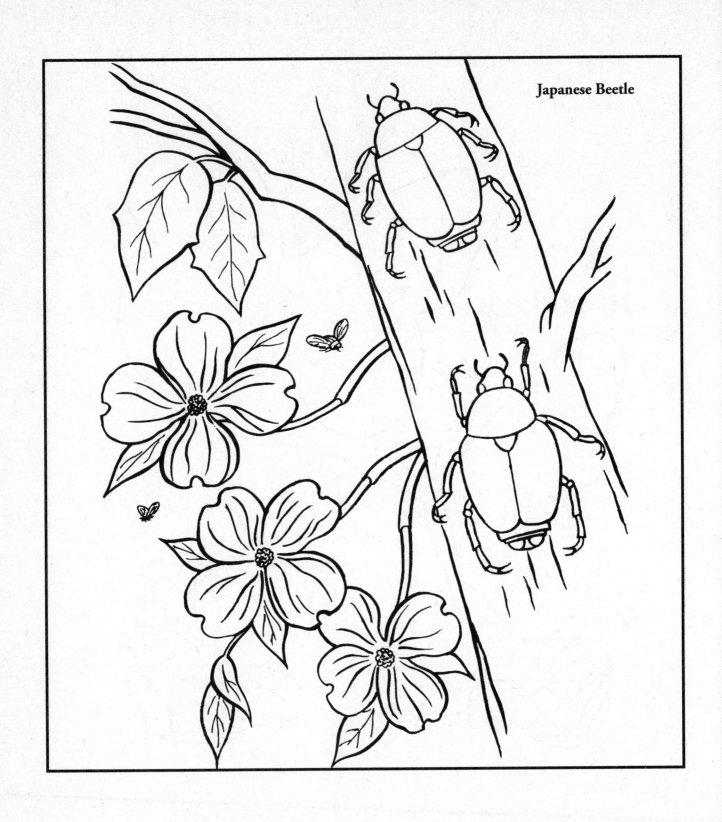

Japanese Beetle

My backyard is full of bugs. God made them all!

Pill Bug

Pill bugs like to hide under old wood.

Ladybug

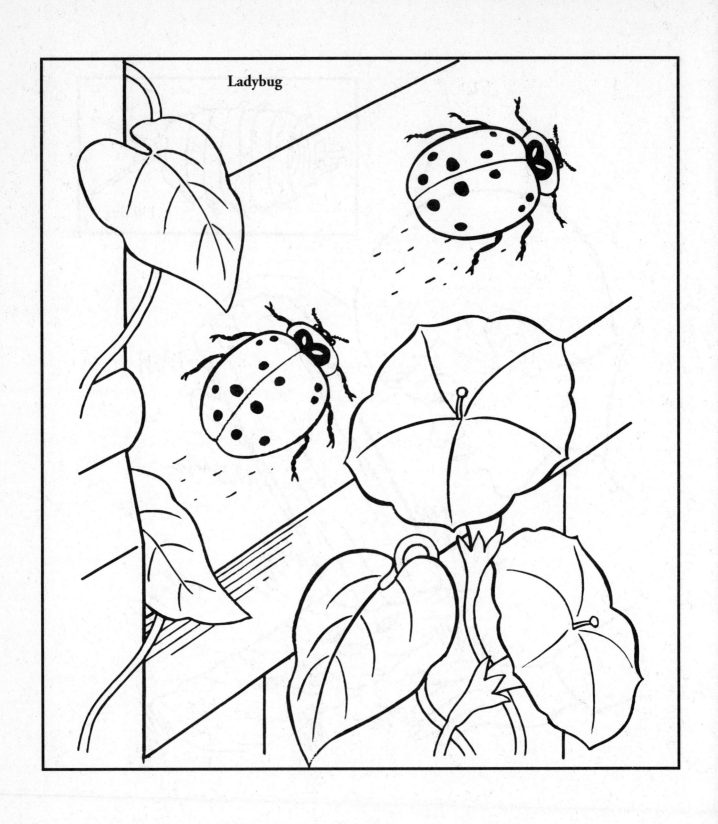

Have you seen a ladybug in your backyard?

Monarch Butterfly Caterpillar

These caterpillars will become beautiful butterflies.

Bumblebee

The bumblebee flies from flower to flower, collecting and spreading pollen.

Connect the dots to see the flower this bumblebee is visiting.

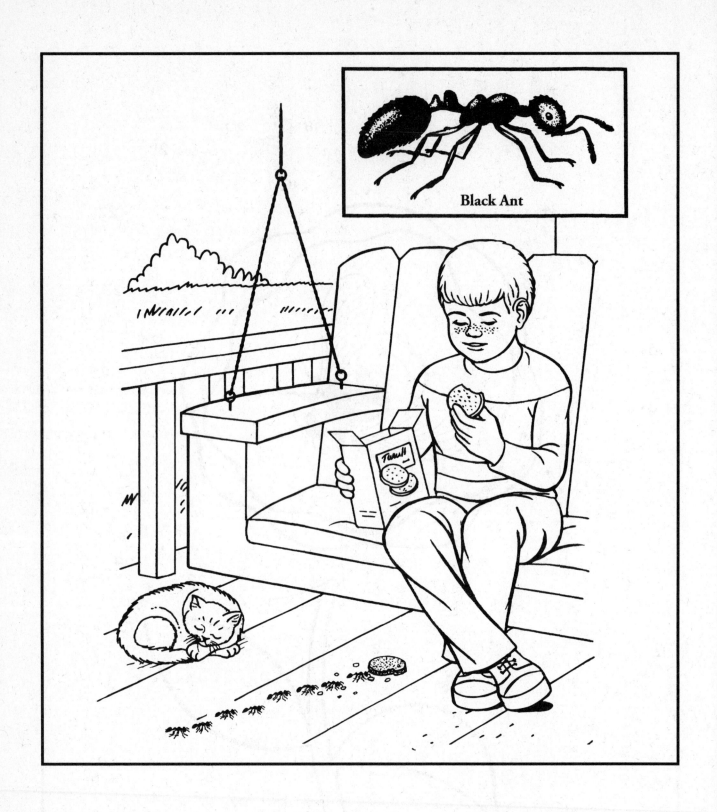

Black Ant

Black ants like to find crumbs.

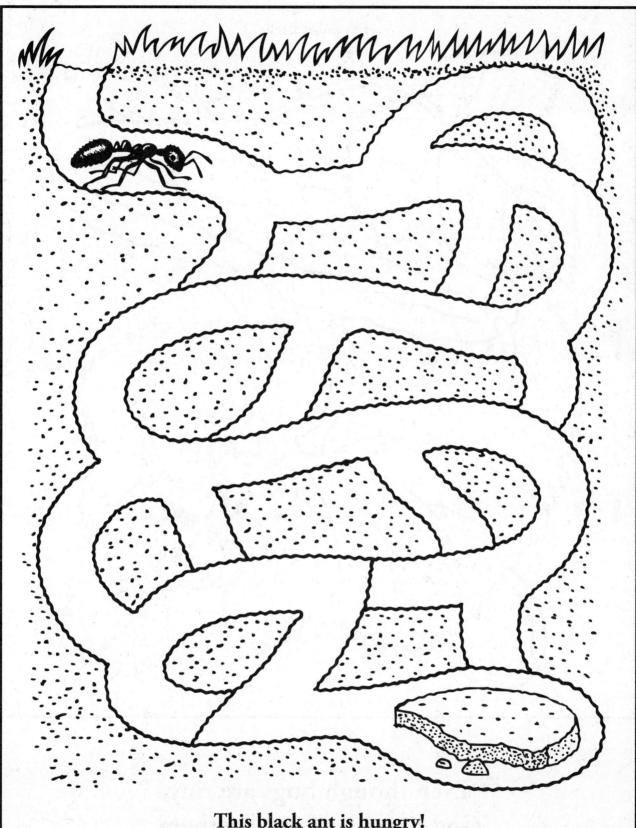

This black ant is hungry!
Help him find his way home to his snack.

Cucumber Beetle

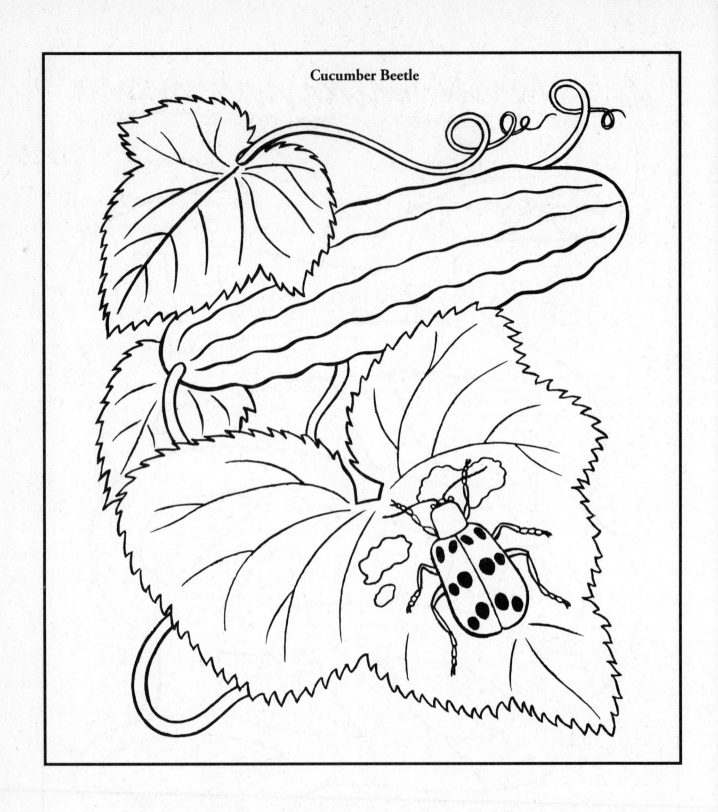

**Even though bugs are tiny,
God provides food for them.**

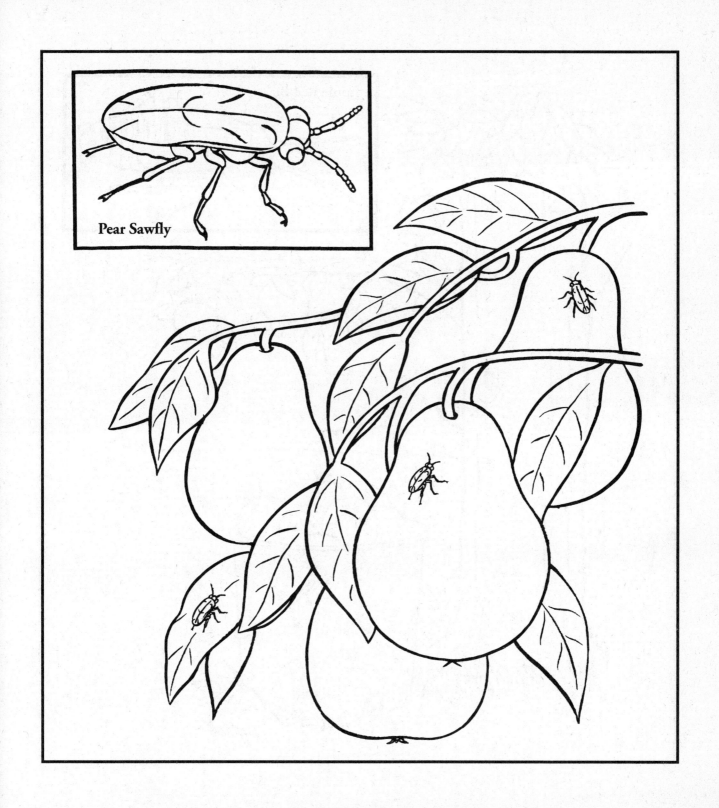

Pear Sawfly

What do you think this bug likes to eat?

Apple Red Bug

Do you like to eat apples? So does this bug.

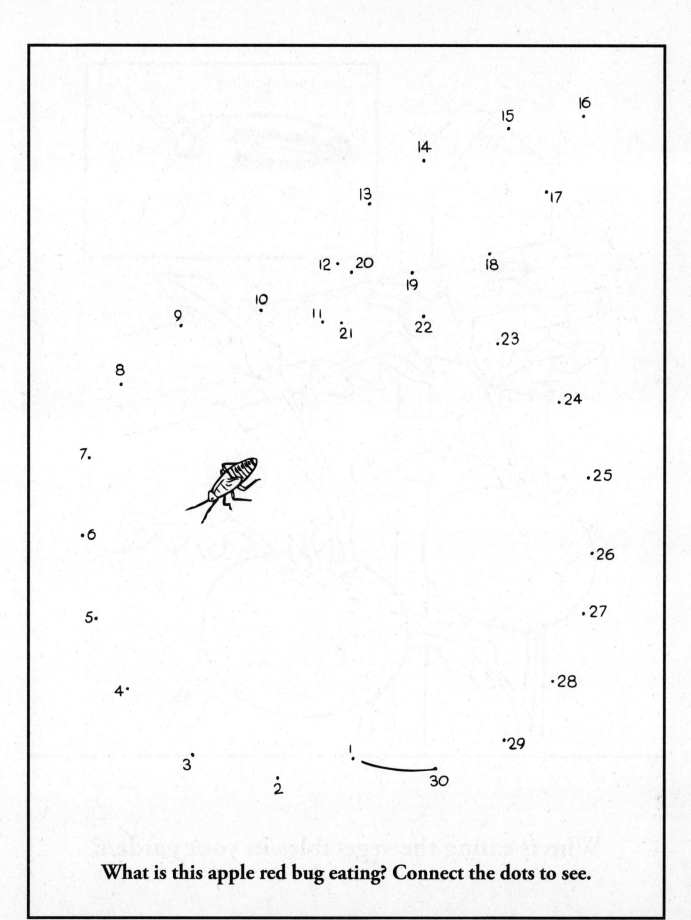

What is this apple red bug eating? Connect the dots to see.

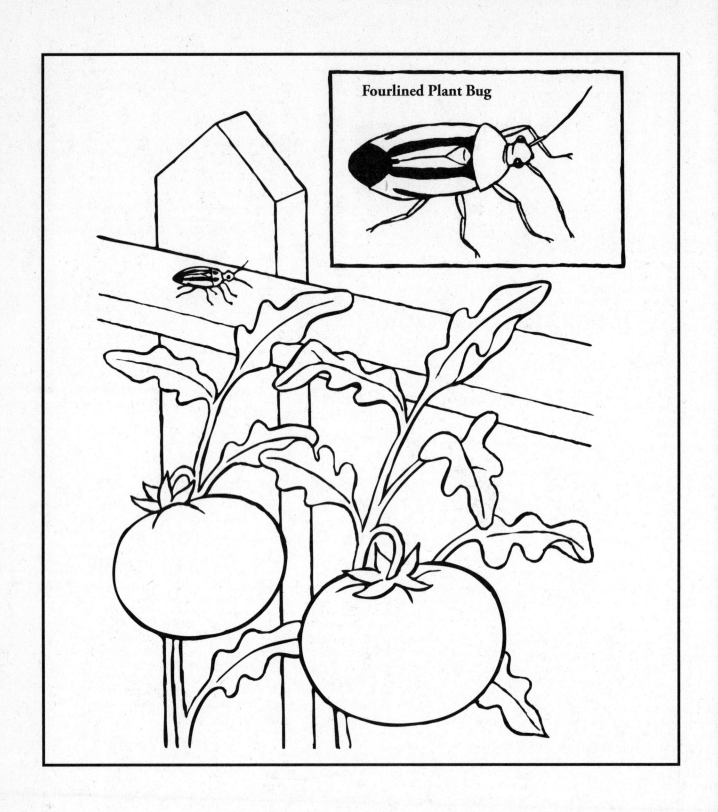

Fourlined Plant Bug

Who is eating the vegetables in your garden?

Redbanded Leafhopper

A leafhopper bug likes lettuce.

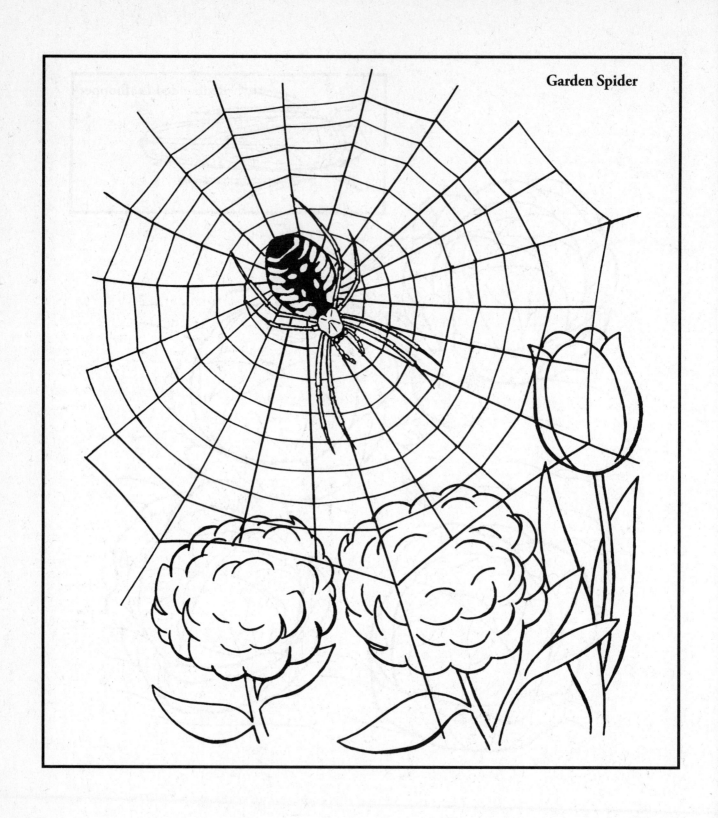

This garden spider eats bugs!

Help this garden spider find her friends.

```
D L E A F H O P P E R
R K L M N O P Q R E A
A N I K M A B B S B T
G R A S S H O P P E R
O C N T W Y S W M L N
N I L G E L T E E B U
F T T R J Z Y D C M I
L O H E G I E H O U V
Y L D E W S F G X B S
R B U T T E R F L Y W
```

GRASSHOPPER

BUTTERFLY

LEAFHOPPER

DRAGONFLY

BUMBLEBEE

BEETLE

Can you find the names of bugs in this word search?
Look up, down, across, and backwards.

There are 3 bugs hiding on this page.
Circle the bugs you find.

Dragonfly

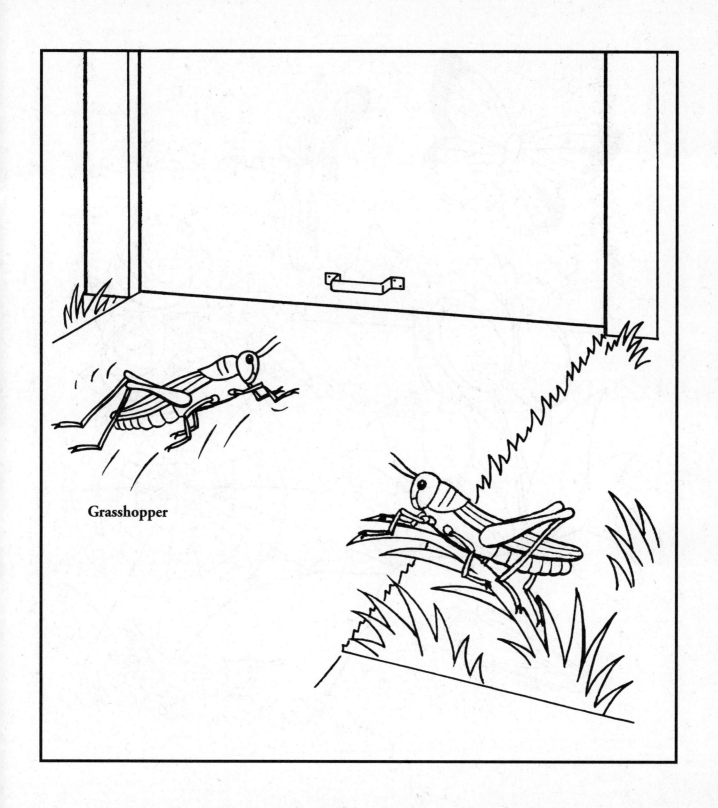

Grasshopper

Grasshoppers are strong jumpers.

"The earth is full of the things you made."

Psalm 104:13

Dinosaurs!

Triceratops was named for the
three horns on his head.

Anatosaurus had a bill like a duck.

**Stegosaurus used the spikes on his tail
to scare off his enemies.**

Something is missing!
Connect the dots to see how Stegosaurus fought off his enemies.

**Apatosaurus is also called Brontosaurus,
which means "thunder lizard."**

Help Apatosaurus get back to her nest.

Iguanodon had spikes on his hands.

**Scelidosaurus had spiked armor
on his back for protection.**

**Ankylosaurus whipped his tail like
a club to keep enemies away.**

Styrocosaurus was an armored dinosaur.

Stegoceras had a thick, bony head.

CLAWS   **FOSSILS**

REPTILE   **TEETH**

EGGS   **ARMOR**

```
Z A F O S S I L S
P C B O D N C D X
E J R I N C T Q A
L A B K J L E R R
I L T H I A F S M
T M E N Q W G M O
P T E G G S R S R
E V T O P G F K Y
R V H W E L J H I
```

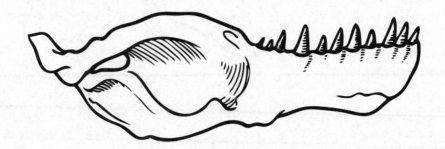

Find these dinosaur words in the puzzle.
Look up, down, and across.

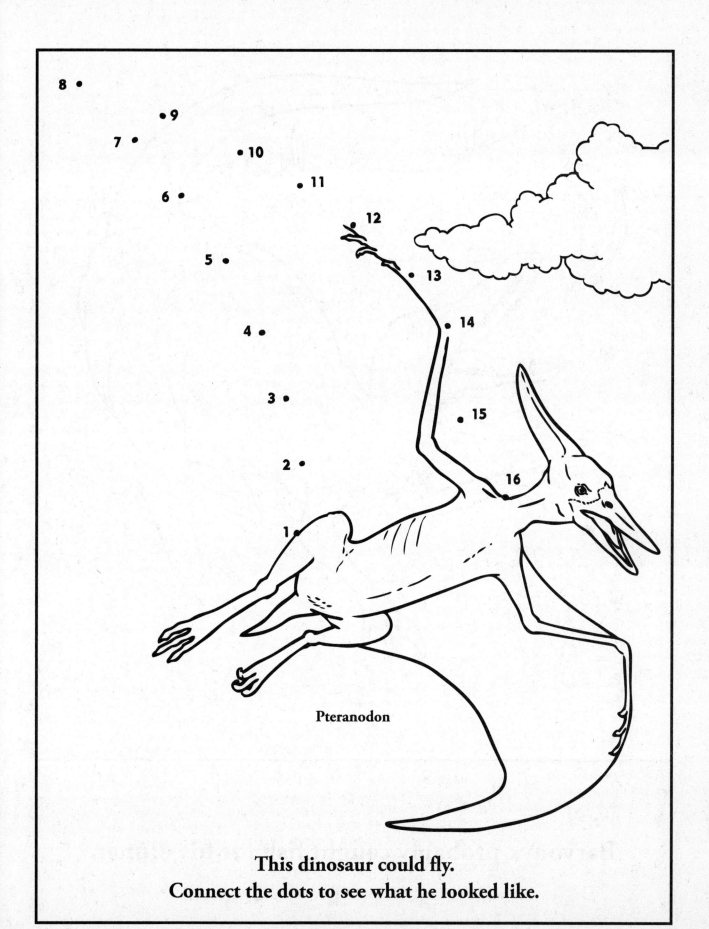

This dinosaur could fly.
Connect the dots to see what he looked like.

Baryonyx probably caught fish for his dinner.

Deinonychus had huge claws!

Oviraptor's name means "egg thief."

Connect the dots to see what Oviraptor is having for dinner.

Velociraptor was a very fast runner.

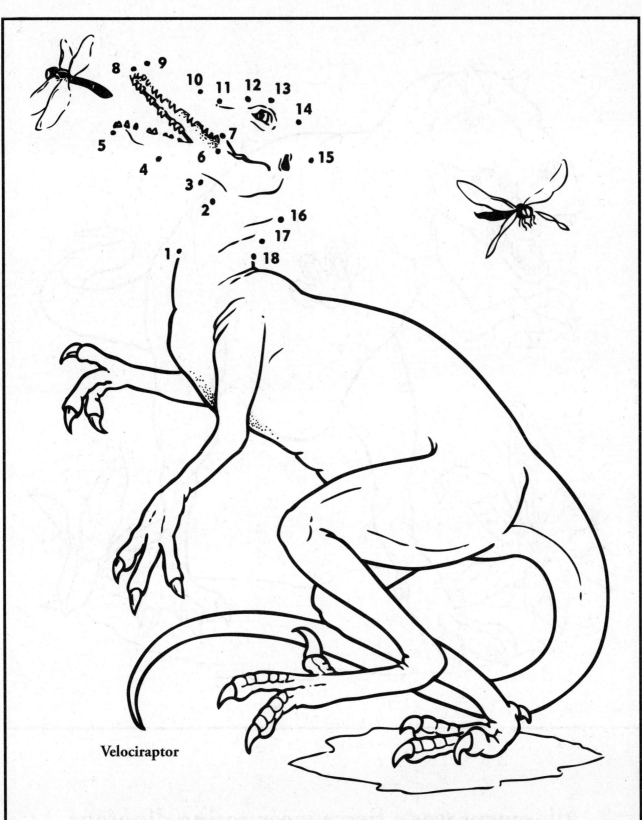

8   9
10   11   12   13
14
7
5
6   15
4
3
2
16
17
1   18

Velociraptor

This dragonfly is about to be some dinosaur's dinner!
Connect the dots to see which one.

Allosaurus was a fierce meat-eating dinosaur.

Help Hypsilophodon escape from Allosaurus!

Tyrannosaurus Rex had big, sharp teeth!

What amazing animals God made!

"With your wisdom you made them all."

Psalm 104:24

God Made Outer Space

"In the beginning God created the sky and the earth."

Genesis 1:1

God made planet Earth.

He made other planets too.

"He counts the stars and names each one."

Psalm 147:4

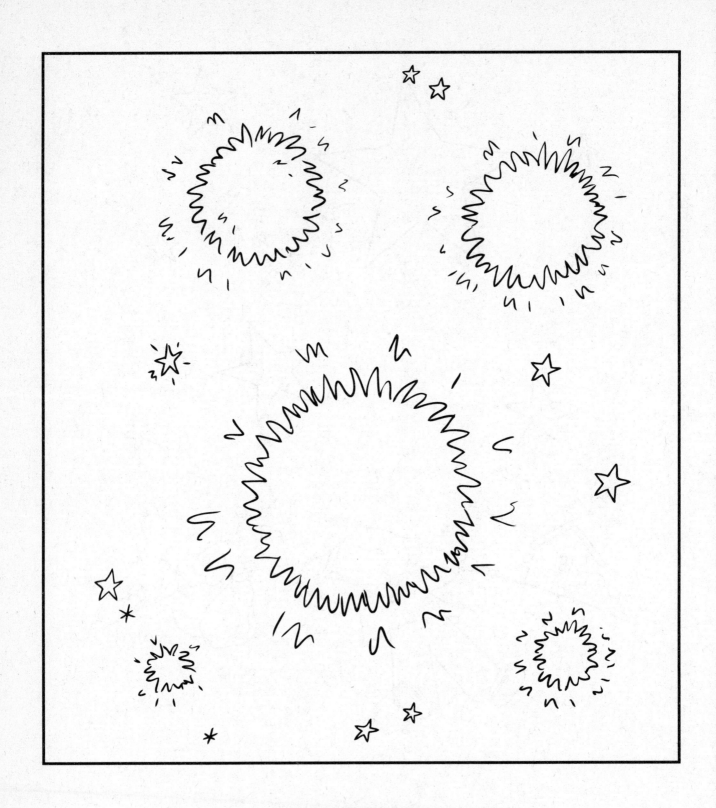

Stars are colorful, bright balls that give off heat and light.

The sun that shines on Earth is a yellow star.

**Constellations are pictures in the sky.
One is Leo, the Lion.**

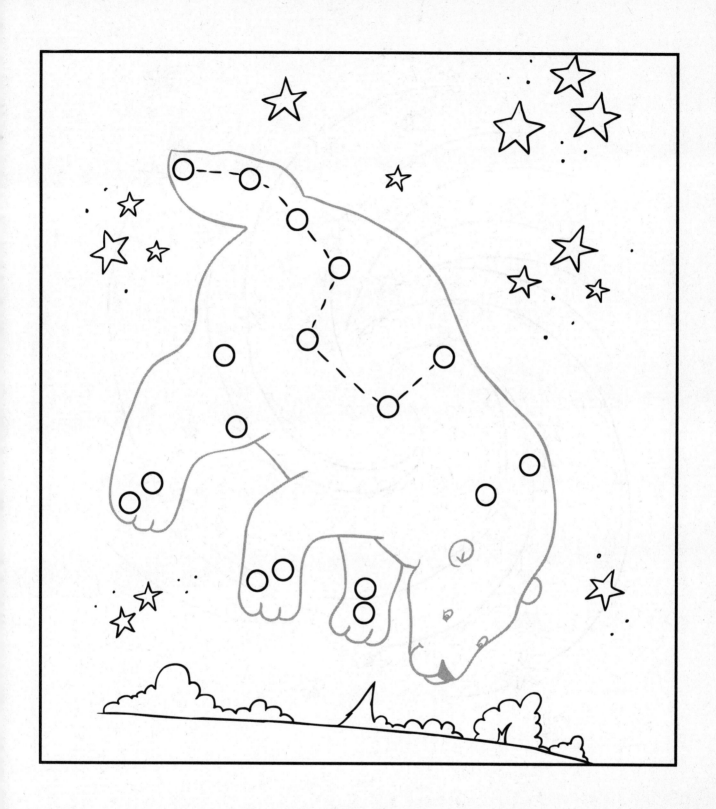

Another constellation is the Great Bear.

**Galaxies contain many stars and planets.
Our galaxy is the Milky Way.**

God made the moon that gives light to Earth at night.

**Comets are balls of dust and ice.
A comet can have a long tail.**

Meteoroids and asteroids are space rocks.

**Space explorers wear space suits to
keep them warm and safe.**

**Robots, rovers, shuttles, and rockets
help us explore outer space.**

"Even the highest heavens are his."

Deuteronomy 10:14

God Made Me

"God created human beings."

Genesis 1:27

Thank you, God, for my legs.

Thank you, God, for my feet.

Thank you, God, for my arms.

Thank you, God, for my hands.

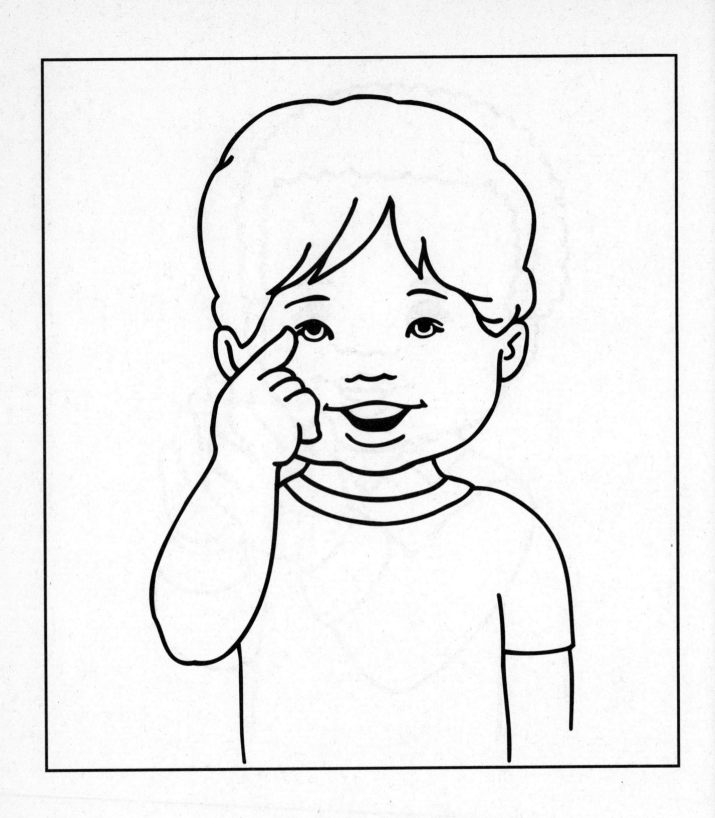

Thank you, God, for my eyes.

Thank you, God, for my ears.

Thank you, God, for my nose.

Thank you, God, for my mouth.

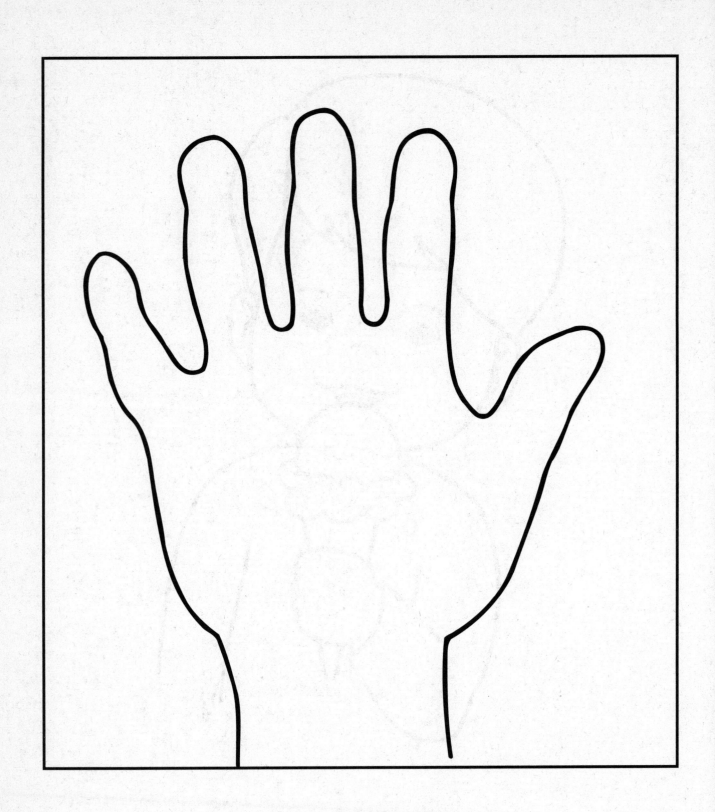

God made my hands.

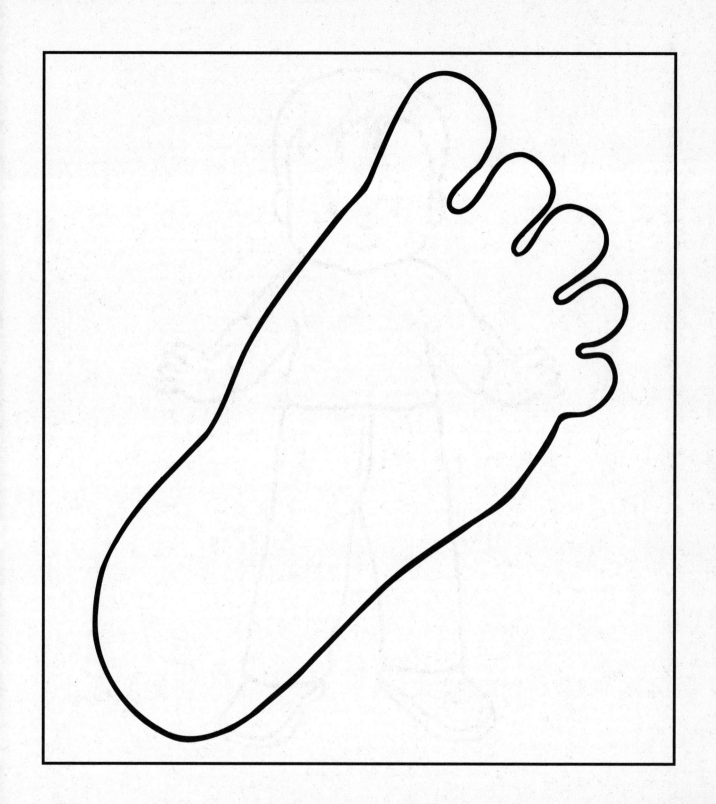

God made my feet.

God made my arms.

God made my legs.

Thank you, God, for making me.

"You made me in an amazing and wonderful way."

Psalm 139:14

Pets Are Fun

Pets are for loving.

"A good man takes care of his animals."

Proverbs 12:10

Kittens like to play with balls.

So do puppies.

A healthy pony needs lots of good food.

My guinea pig makes me laugh.

"Let the water be filled with living things."

Genesis 1:20

A hamster likes a soft bed.

My parrot can talk!

A turtle carries his house on his back.

My bunny's name is Isabella.

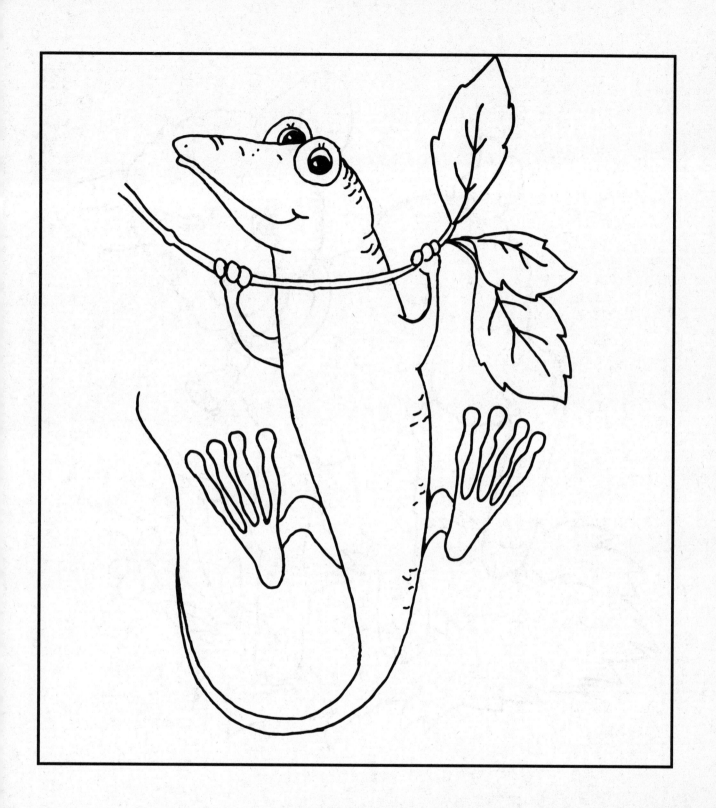

A lizard likes a leafy branch.

"Let the earth be filled with animals."

This gerbil is hungry!

"God saw that this was good."

Genesis 1:21

God's Underwater Animals

"He created every living thing that moves in the sea."

Genesis 1:21

God made the manatee.

God made puffer fish.

God made the sea horse.

Whee!

God made penguins.

God made the lobster.

God made eels.

God made the octopus.

God made the seal.

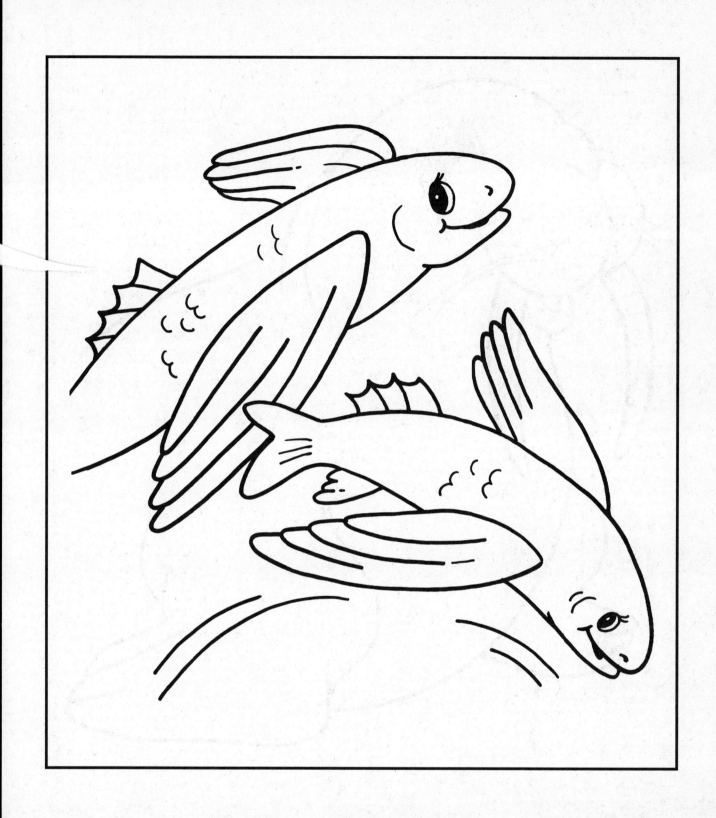

God made flying fish.

God made the walrus.

"Praise him, you large sea animals and all the oceans."

Psalm 148:7

Puppies and Kittens

God is good.

Jesus cares.

Love one another.

Praise the Lord!

God bless you.

God loves you.

Love never ends.

Smile, God loves you!

Be kind.

Rejoice in the Lord!

Bible Animals

donkey

sheep

bear

camel

sparrow

COW

rooster

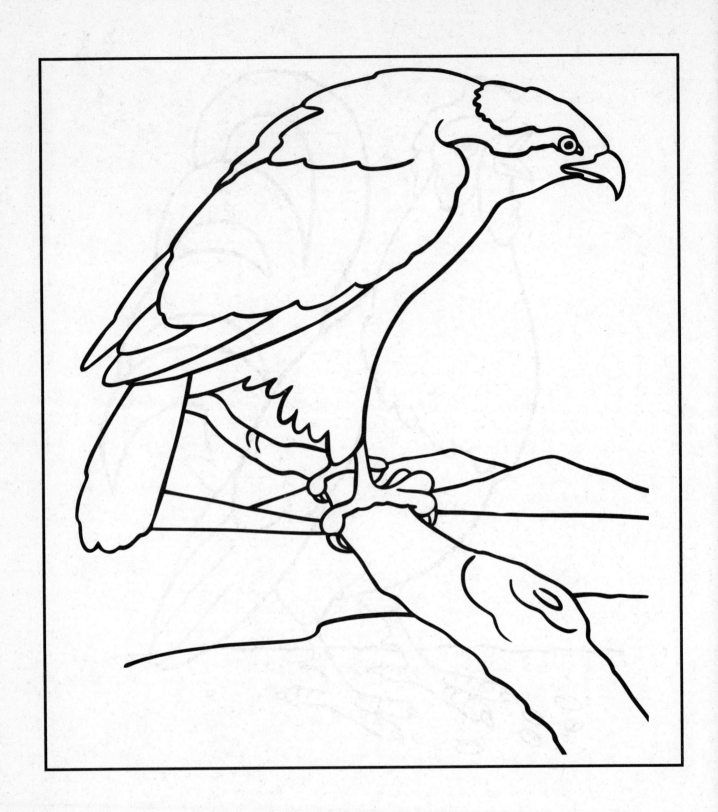

eagle

raven

fox

goat

dove

frog

deer

God made all the animals.

God's Animals Friends

God made all of the animals, and they
make different sounds.

What does each animal say?

The lion says, "Roar!"

The horse says, "Neigh!"

The snake says, "Sssss."

The cat says, "Meow."

The dog says, "Ruff!"

The pig says, "Oink."

The duck says, "Quack."

The sheep says, "Baaaa!"

The rooster says, "Cockadoodledoo!"

The bear says, "Grrr!"

The bee says, "Bzzzz."

The robin says, "Cheep."

"God said, 'Let the earth be filled with animals.'"

Genesis 1:24

Creation

plants

flowers

trees

sun

moon and stars

dolphin

octopus

penguin

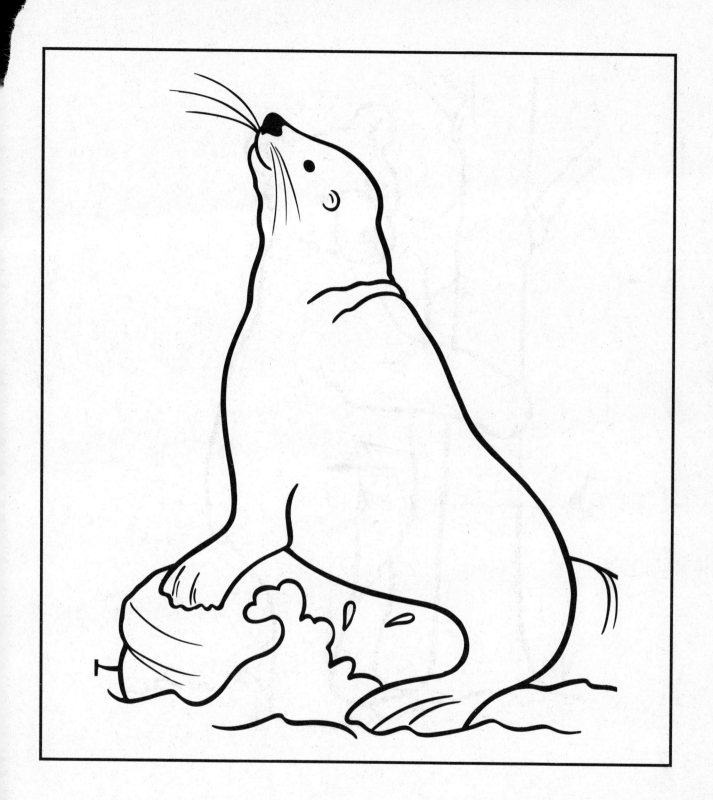

seal

bear

deer

"God looked at everything he had made, and it was very good.'"

Genesis 1:31